★ *GREAT SPORTS TEAMS* ★

THE ATLANTA

BASEBALL TEAM

Thomas S. Owens

Enslow Publishers, Inc.

44 Fadem Road   PO Box 38
Box 699   Aldershot
Springfield, NJ 07081   Hants GU12 6BP
USA   UK

Dedication

Thanks to Diana Star Helmer, a brave fan.

Library of Congress Cataloging-in-Publication Data

Owens, Tom, 1960–
    The Atlanta Braves baseball team / Thomas S. Owens.
        p. cm. — (Great sports teams)
    Includes bibliographical references and index.
    Summary: A team history of the Atlanta Braves, from their start in Boston through their championship seasons in the 1990s, focusing on notable players and important front office figures.
    ISBN 0-7660-1021-X
    1. Atlanta Braves (Baseball team)—History—Juvenile literature. [1. Atlanta Braves (Baseball team)—History. 2. Baseball—History.] I. Title. II. Series.
GV875.A8094 1998
796.357'64'09758231—dc21   97-19145
                                                             CIP
                                                             AC

Printed in the United States of America

10 9 8 7 6 5 4 3 2 1

Illustration Credits: AP/Wide World Photos, pp. 4, 7, 8, 10, 13, 14, 16, 19, 20, 22, 25, 26, 28, 31, 32, 34, 37, 38.

Cover Illustration: AP/Wide World Photos.

CONTENTS

*A*fter pitching the Braves to a 3-2 win in Game 1 of the 1995 World Series, Greg Maddux suffered a 5-4 loss in Game 5.

THE FALL CLASSIC

n 1995 the Braves faced a strange problem. The team went into Game 6 of the 1995 Fall Classic needing only one win for its first world championship in thirty years of Atlanta history. The fans had strange on-and-off feelings about the team. The Braves were making their third World Series appearance in five years. No one argued about their place as a National League powerhouse.

However, the team was zero for two in previous tries for the World Series trophy. Some fans wondered if bad luck haunted the Braves. In 1993 the Phillies outlasted Atlanta in the National League Championship Series, denying the team a World Series return. Even worse, the Braves were on track to win a wild-card berth for the 1994 postseason. Yet they couldn't contend for a World Series spot—no team could. A players' strike canceled the event. It was the first time since 1904 that the World Series was not held.

Now Atlanta right fielder David Justice seemed to place another curse on his team. The Braves returned to Georgia after the fifth game of the Series in Cleveland. Justice's teammate, pitching ace Greg Maddux, had been hammered by the Indians for a 5-4 loss. Wouldn't Justice be happier playing back home in front of friendlier fans?

Obviously not. "They'll probably burn our houses down if we don't win," he said of Atlanta fans, in words that were reprinted and rebroadcast around the world. "They're not behind us like the Cleveland fans, who were standing and cheering even when they were three runs down."[1] Justice was mad at more than local fans. He was mad at himself. Justice had been hitless in the previous game, and owned only 3 hits in 18 previous at bats.

During the regular season, Justice's .253 average was the lowest of his career. Suddenly reporters talked more about Justice's marriage to movie actress Halle Berry than his hitting. Of course, many journalists had never gotten along with the 1990 Rookie of the Year, who often didn't want to be bothered by the media after games. Likewise, Justice ignored many autograph seekers in Atlanta. Neither group seemed likely to forgive him soon.

Atlanta fans voiced their feelings about Justice during his first at bat. The Atlanta-Fulton County Stadium stands, jammed with 51,875 spectators, had many booing critics. Justice's loudest put-downs had been shouted before the game started, with the

*A*tlanta Braves right fielder David Justice yells as he rounds the bases after his solo homer in the sixth inning of Game 6 of the World Series at Atlanta-Fulton County Stadium.

announcement of his name. Meanwhile, Justice didn't issue a reply until the sixth inning. Against lefty Jim Poole, Justice cracked a home run over the right field fence. The run would be the only score of the game on either side.

As Justice trotted around the bases, he pumped his right fist in the air. Was his face a show of anger or an expression holding back tears? Some fans thought the outfielder's display was a player overflowing with happiness. Some reporters thought the gesture was simply a sign of relief.

How did Justice feel before the game? "My stomach hurt so bad before the game, I didn't eat," he told a reporter. "I thought 50,000 people were going to boo me in the World Series."[2]

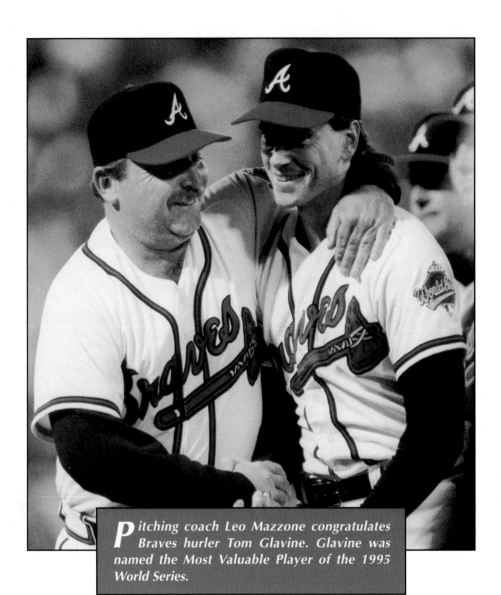

Pitching coach Leo Mazzone congratulates Braves hurler Tom Glavine. Glavine was named the Most Valuable Player of the 1995 World Series.

Braves starting pitcher Tom Glavine added more "justice" to the evening's effort. The left-hander allowed only one hit over eight innings. The final inning was handed to closer Mark Wohlers.

Wohlers was famed for throwing at speeds reaching 100 miles per hour. While he didn't strike out any Cleveland hitters that night, he coaxed three batters in a row into flying out. The last line drive was snared by center fielder Marquis Grissom, who had fueled the Braves with a record 25 hits through three rounds of post-season play. With defensive help, the flame-throwing Wohlers had maintained Glavine's one-hitter and 1-0 victory. Only four times before in World Series history had a team won while allowing its foes only one hit.

Wohlers, Glavine, and Justice shared a unique history after the victory. The three were among only ten members of the first pennant-winning Braves team of 1991 who remained to share in the World Series crown four years later.

The World Series Most Valuable Player Award (MVP) went to Glavine. Meanwhile, fans forgave Justice, if the celebration parade days later was any clue. More than six hundred thousand Braves' supporters crowded Peachtree Street. The team snaked down a two-mile route through Atlanta, before presenting its trophy to the city at the ballpark. On the route, a huge banner flapped in the breeze. "Justice Is Done" read the sign.

*W*alter "Rabbit" Maranville was the star player of the 1914 "Miracle Braves."

FINDING A HOME

The Braves are the only team to win a World Series while representing three different cities. The first club played in Boston beginning in 1871 under an assortment of nicknames such as the Red Stockings, Doves, Rustlers, Bees, and Red Caps. Harry Wright, founder of the 1869 Cincinnati Red Stockings (considered by many to be baseball's first organized team of paid players), started the Boston team with three former Reds players. Boston was one of the first eight teams that formed the National League in 1876.

An early version of the Braves was known as the "Beaneaters." Despite the name, they captured eight pennants before 1900. From 1906 to 1910, the Dovey brothers owned the team, making them the "Doves." Then, in 1914, the team soared from last place in July to first, sweeping the favored Philadelphia Athletics in four straight World Series games.

In 1914 the Braves began the year by losing 18 of 22 games, and then ended the season with 60 wins out of its last 76 games. The team became the "Miracle Braves" to newspapers and the city of Boston.

Hard Times

By 1918, however, the team's attendance and record was slipping. The Braves were never contenders throughout the 1920s.

As losing became a habit for the Braves, the team struggled financially. Boston signed an overweight, over-the-hill Babe Ruth in 1935. The team knew that the city remembered Ruth more than fifteen years earlier as a talented Boston Red Sox pitcher. He was there to get a few more fans in the stands—and a few more mentions in newspapers. Instead, the team's record, 38-115, made history.

Boston lost so many games in the 1940s, they tried changing their name to "Bees" to bring back fans. Still, the team couldn't win away fans from the cross-town Red Sox until 1948, when the Braves became National League champions. "Spahn, Sain and Two Days of Rain" became the battle cry of fans because the team's starting pitching success depended mainly on hurlers Warren Spahn and Johnny Sain. The Braves lost to the Indians in the World Series, a reversal of what would happen nearly fifty years later.

Sam Jethroe became the Braves' first African-American player in 1950. He responded by winning the National League's Rookie of the Year award, and

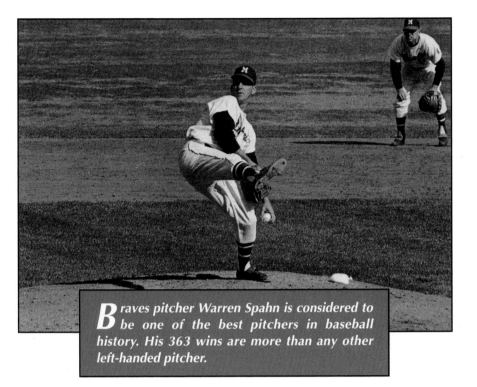

*B*raves pitcher Warren Spahn is considered to be one of the best pitchers in baseball history. His 363 wins are more than any other left-handed pitcher.

leading the league in stolen bases each of his first two seasons.

Yet whenever the club's record faded, so did public support. In 1953 owner Lou Perini said goodbye to Boston and moved the team to Milwaukee.

Winning in Wisconsin

Milwaukee already loved the Milwaukee Brewers, one of the Braves' minor league teams. They welcomed the parent team, and in just four years, Perini's gamble paid off. The Milwaukee Braves are remembered as world champions in 1957, who defeated the much-favored New York Yankees. Lew Burdette, traded from the Yankees and remembered

Finding a Home

*P*hil Niekro first joined the Braves in 1964. Famous for his knuckleball, Niekro baffled major-league hitters for 24 seasons.

as an alleged spitballer, pitched three complete-game Series wins against the Yankees.

One unlikely hero of 1957 was Bob "Hurricane" Hazle. Three years earlier, a storm named "Hazel" had rampaged the East Coast. Hazle's hitting rampage was just as newsworthy. The minor leaguer nicely batted .403 with 7 homers and 27 RBIs in 41 games.

In a World Series rematch the following year, the Yanks took back their title from the Braves. Yet those two years weren't the only highlights in Milwaukee Braves history. In 1954 the team unveiled a skinny infielder they had purchased from the Negro League Indianapolis Clowns for $7,500. The rookie was Hank Aaron, baseball's future all-time home run king.

Shrinking fan support caused the owners to look for another home, and in 1966 they chose Atlanta. Surprisingly, the team left Milwaukee without a single losing season, the only franchise to have that honor.

Old Team, New Ways

Relocated in Georgia, the Atlanta Braves would win their first division title in three years, only to lose to the 1969 New York "Miracle Mets" in the first year of the newly-devised Championship Series. Atlanta wouldn't end a season in first place again until 1982.

Braves' history grew in a different direction in 1991. In spring training the team signed Atlanta Falcons football star Deion "Prime Time" Sanders. Sanders had starred for the Florida State University Seminoles. Florida fans cheered him with a tomahawk-chop arm wave. Through Sanders, Fulton County Stadium was nicknamed "The Chop Shop."

Braves fans added another tradition, developing a chant. Some Native Americans protested that chanting was disrespectful. Others believed that the team's tomahawk chop was a Native American stereotype. The biggest objection was that the team's name made fun of one race of people.

Former United States President Jimmy Carter attended Atlanta games, joining in the chop cheer. How did he view the protests? "With the Braves on top, we have a brave, successful and courageous team, and I think we can look on the American Indians as brave, successful and attractive," he told reporters.[1]

*H*ank Aaron starts toward first base April 5, 1974 after hitting his 714th career home run to tie Babe Ruth's record. Aaron is the career leader in home runs and RBI.

BRAVE WARRIORS

Whether they were bright spots in gloomy seasons of losses, or shining stars on a field dotted with winners, the Braves has never been short of memorable players.

Rabbit Maranville

The star of the 1914 "Miracle" Braves got his "Rabbit" nickname not for speed, but for looks. The fancy-fielding shortstop, who was small (five-foot five-inches and 155 pounds), but had big ears, said a seven-year-old fan gave him his nickname as a rookie. All but eight of his twenty-three seasons were spent as a Brave. He was known for wacky behavior on and off the field, often sitting on opponents after he tagged them. Maranville was voted into the Hall of Fame in 1954, only months after his death.

Hank Aaron

When Aaron made his professional debut with the Indianapolis Clowns of the Negro American League in 1952, his first manager Buster Haywood offered a simple judgment. "He's a natural-born ballplayer," the skipper said of Aaron. "God done sent me something."[1] Aaron, who played in twenty-four All-Star games, created dozens of hitting records. In honor of baseball's all-time home run king with 755, the city of Atlanta wanted to change the address of Turner Field to "755 Aaron Way." Aaron was elected to the Hall of Fame in 1982.

Warren Spahn

Spahn's 363 wins remain an all-time record for any left-hander in baseball. "Spahnnie" was a league victory leader for eight seasons, collecting 20-win seasons thirteen times. Surprisingly, the Braves had been the only team to scout the teenaged Spahn. Spahn's number, twenty-one, was the first ever retired by the Braves, in 1965. He was chosen for the Hall of Fame in 1973.

Eddie Mathews

This strapping third baseman was the first Braves home run king, becoming only the seventh man in history to surpass 500 homers. Mathews and Hank Aaron combined for 1,267 homers, 60 more than famed teammates Babe Ruth and Lou Gehrig. Mathews was the only player to see action with the Boston, Milwaukee, and Atlanta Braves, and he was also the

The Atlanta Braves Baseball Team

*E*ddie Mathews takes the pitch deep for home run number 400. Mathews would hit over 500 home runs in his Hall of Fame career.

first man to play for, coach, and manage the team. Mathews was enshrined in Cooperstown in 1978.

Phil Niekro

"Knucksie," who was taught the knuckleball by his father, began his career as a reliever. Converted to a starting pitcher, Niekro led the Braves in wins in ten different seasons. As a tribute, Niekro returned to Atlanta in 1987, pitching one late-season "farewell game" at age forty-eight. He returned with more than 300 career wins. Younger brother Joe pitched as Phil's teammate in 1973–74. Together, the brothers won a record 539 games. Niekro was inducted into the Hall of Fame in 1997.

*T*he Braves starting pitchers of 1993; (left to right) Tom Glavine, Greg Maddux, Pete Smith, John Smoltz, and Steve Avery. Glavine, Maddux, and Smoltz are Cy Young winners.

Dale Murphy

Originally a catcher in his early career, Murphy developed a mental block and couldn't throw the ball back to the pitcher regularly. For basestealers, he'd often overthrow to the outfield. A move to center field in 1980 made the difference. In six straight seasons as a starter, "Murph" never dipped below 29 homers a year. He earned five Gold Gloves for fielding excellence, and consecutive Most Valuable Player awards in 1982–83.

Greg Maddux

After the 1995 season, Maddux was dubbed "Mad Dog" by his teammates, when he led the National League with a 19-2 record and 1.63 ERA. To his credit, Maddux didn't brag. "There's always room for improvement," he told the media.[2] In 1996, Maddux was 15-11 with a 2.72 ERA, and added a seventh straight Gold Glove for fielding. In the National League Championship Series (NLCS), Maddux allowed only six hits and one run in the clinching win against St. Louis. In the second game of the World Series, he held the Yankees scoreless on six hits through eight innings. Maddux offsets his lack of speed with amazing control, and has the guts to throw any of four different pitches any place in the strike zone at any time in the count.

Tom Glavine

When the Braves chose him in the second round of the 1994 free-agent (amateur) draft, Glavine was also a fourth-round pick by the Los Angeles Kings of the National Hockey League. Glavine chose the diamond over the rink. Yet in 1988, his first full season with the Braves, Glavine was anything but great. He finished the year at 7-17.

His career blossomed in 1991, with Glavine winning the Cy Young Award as the league's top pitcher. Glavine became only the second pitcher in Atlanta history to win 20 games, finishing at 20-11. In 1996 Glavine became the first team member to write a book, *None But the Braves*.

*A*tlanta Braves owner Ted Turner can often be seen by the dugout supporting his team. To the right is his wife, actress Jane Fonda.

THE CHIEF MINDS

The Braves became the toast of 1990s baseball through the performances of three men. Surprisingly, none of them ever played an inning for the team.

Ted Turner III

At the top of the list of people who transformed Atlanta from a pretender to a contender is R. E. "Ted" Turner III. Back in 1976, when Turner bought the Braves, some disbelievers thought the fast-talking television station bigwig wanted the team only to turn a quick buck. At first, he only wanted to broadcast the team's games on his growing cable station. However, he guessed that owning the team would be an easier way to get broadcast rights, prompting the now-bargain purchase of the Braves for $11 million.

This owner had no baseball experience, but soon surprised other team officials. He was at the ballpark constantly, participating in on-field promotions such as ostrich races. Turner even tried managing the Braves for one game in 1977. To get more fans to buy tickets, Turner wanted to prove that the Braves were fun.

Turner was serious, too, in turning the Braves into a winner. He began offering millions of dollars in multi-year contracts to free agents; veteran players who had earned the right to choose the team they would play with.

Bobby Cox

One of the first major additions Turner made to the team was in the 1978 choice of Bobby Cox. Never before had Cox managed in the majors. Cox had been in the Braves organization briefly as a player. He began as a Dodgers minor leaguer for seven years, before joining the Braves' triple-A team in 1967. That December he was traded to the Yankees. In the majors, Cox was a starting third baseman for the 1968 Yankees. He played part-time in New York in 1969, his last year in the big leagues. By 1971 the thirty-year-old was retired due to knee problems.

After his 1978 appointment, Cox made slow but steady progress in leading the Braves. By 1980 the team was 81-80—the first time since 1974 that they had a winning record. Cox was fired after 1981 ended. A players' strike had marred the season, which had seen Atlanta's attendance dip by more than a half-million. Joe Torre became the new manager, partly because he enjoyed past fame as a Milwaukee and Atlanta Braves star of the 1960s. Toronto quickly hired

The Atlanta Braves Baseball Team

B raves manager Bobby Cox scratches his head in the dugout in the fifth inning of a World Series game against the Toronto Blue Jays.

Cox, and Cox developed the Blue Jays into a solid contender over the next four seasons.

Turner rehired Cox for 1986, this time as a general manager. Cox was credited with supervising the players who would grow into 1990s stars, namely the talented young hurlers such as Tom Glavine and John Smoltz. When Cox was reseated as Braves manager in June 1990, the team still needed a smart judge of talent as general manager. Given the choice between his two old jobs for 1991, Cox grabbed the on-field duty, leaving the "upstairs" work behind.

*B*raves general manager John Schuerholz (left) and team president Stan Kasten (right) talk to reporters after the Braves 1995 World Series victory over the Cleveland Indians.

John Schuerholz

Turner stepped in once more, signing John Schuerholz away from the Kansas City Royals to become the Braves' general manager. Schuerholz began in baseball as a scouting assistant with the Orioles in 1966. He had moved to Kansas City in 1968, where he helped find the players who became the first Royals in 1969.

Schuerholz grew up professionally with the Royals. He was only forty-one in 1981, when he became the team's executive vice president and general manager. Schuerholz did more than find and keep good players in Kansas City. He oversaw many business details, including the amount of money the organization spent.

The Atlanta Braves Baseball Team

After twenty-three years in Kansas City, Schuerholz described why he left. "I was with Kansas City when we built an expansion franchise," he explained. "I thought the challenge of coming to Atlanta and helping re-establish this organization would certainly be energizing and invigorating."[1] Some reporters joked that the Braves would become the "Royals of the South."

When he came to Atlanta in 1991, Schuerholz wanted many changes quickly. He hired new groundskeepers to improve the look and feel of the field. He wanted better food and souvenir selections. Yet the new executive had no complaints about the talent of field manager Cox. While at Kansas City, Schuerholz had wanted to hire Cox to manage the Royals!

Cox refused to brag about himself, even after leading the Braves to a second straight World Series appearance in 1992. "All I do is fill out the lineup card each day, then sit back and hope it all works out," he told reporters. "Nothing genius about that. Why, sometimes, I just feel lucky to have a job."[2]

Even though the Yankees manhandled the Braves for four straight losses after Atlanta won the first two World Series games of 1996, Cox still had a job. After the season ended, *Forbes* magazine announced estimates of the 400 richest people in America. They ranked Turner the 47th wealthiest, having approximately $2.1 billion. More than owning the National Basketball Association Hawks, the Cable News Network (CNN), Superstation WTBS, and the Braves, Turner ended the year with a lasting place in baseball history. The team's new ballpark will be named Turner Field.

R on Gant was one of the Atlanta Braves star players in the early 1990s. Gant was the first player in Braves' history to have back-to-back "30/30" seasons.

THE 90's DYNASTY

Were the first four Atlanta teams to make World Series appearances in the 1990s that different? Though the Braves were consistent pennant winners in the 1990s, the decade became one of great change for Atlanta. The team ended 1990 with the worst record in the major leagues, just 65 wins.

Change started for the Braves in June 1990. General manager Bobby Cox hadn't been a field manager since serving Toronto in 1985. To start rebuilding the team, Cox was asked to do both jobs.

Cox admitted that he liked the on-field duty better than judging players from the stands. When Cox first took over, he promoted minor-league pitching coach Leo Mazzone to do the same job in Atlanta. Mazzone had helped young pitchers Tom Glavine, John Smoltz, and Steve Avery in the minors. Maybe he could do the same in the majors.

1991

New general manager John Schuerholz provided Cox with a fresh collection of talent in 1991. Free agent first baseman Sid Bream, shortstop Rafael Belliard, and third baseman Terry Pendleton were added to reduce the 158 errors—the most in the National League— made by the previous year's team. Even so, the Braves didn't seem that much luckier in 1991, when the team was nine and a half games behind the division-leading Dodgers at the All-Star break.

At midseason, the happiest news was that pitcher Tom Glavine was 12-4, good enough to be starting the All-Star game. Yet Glavine was the only all-star representative of the Braves. General Manager Schuerholz wanted to help. He succeeded by suggesting that pitcher John Smoltz would have a more positive attitude after sessions with an Atlanta sports psychologist.

The team sailed to the playoffs as outfielder Ron Gant became the first player in Braves' history to earn two consecutive "30/30" seasons, surpassing the mark in both home runs and stolen bases. Glavine became the team's first twenty-game winner since Phil Niekro in 1979. The saddest moment came when Otis Nixon, who had set a team record with 72 stolen bases, was suspended for drug use a month before the season's end. The Braves faced and fell to the Minnesota Twins in the World Series, with the 1991 trophy going to a team that had finished dead last the year before.

The Series had come down to the 10th inning of the seventh game, resulting in a 1-0 win for Minnesota.

*D*eion "Prime Time" Sanders provided the Braves with an offensive spark during the 1992 World Series. His batting average for the series was .533.

At a post-Series parade in Atlanta, one banner-waving fan told the Braves to keep trying. "It's Better to Have Chopped and Lost," said the sign, "Than Never to Have Chopped at All!"[1]

1992

The 1992 Braves returned for a second straight World Series with few new faces. Never before had an Atlanta team won 98 games. As late as May 27, the team was in last place. However, a 13-game winning streak in July (tying the 1982 record) set the team straight.

The pitching twosome of Glavine, with another 20-win season, and Smoltz, who led the National League

*F*red McGriff was the Braves' most dangerous home run threat for many years. McGriff could be counted on to hit close to thirty home runs a year.

with 215 strikeouts, carried the team. A third starring repeater was Gant, notching another outstanding effort, while the entire team's 138 homers topped the league.

Atlanta exhausted itself in the postseason, needing a full seven games to defeat Pittsburgh in the league championship series. Glavine threw a four-hitter to give the Braves a good start in the World Series opener against Toronto.

However, the Blue Jays replied with three straight one-run wins. A grand slam by Lonnie Smith kept the Braves alive with a fifth-game win. Toronto ended Atlanta's dreams with a 4-3 extra-inning win to end the Series in six games.

1993

The 1993 Braves came back with 104 wins, but were beaten by the Phillies in six National League Championship Series games. The bittersweet end offset a storybook season, when a league record 3,884,720 fans flocked to Atlanta. Philadelphia expected a worn-out Braves team, which didn't win its division until the last day of the season. Atlanta saw major changes that July, when slugging first baseman Fred McGriff was swapped from San Diego. On the day he arrived at Fulton County Stadium, the ballpark pressbox caught on fire, as did the team. Greg Maddux, who had been hired away from the Cubs after winning the 1992 Cy Young Award in Chicago, came to win another in Atlanta.

1995

The new arrivals in 1995 were centerfielder Marquis Grissom, and Larry "Chipper" Jones, who took over third base from Terry Pendleton, a free-agent acquisition of the Marlins. Jones finished second in the Rookie of the Year balloting, and became popular for wearing his stirrup socks higher than other players.

Jones summed up the attitude which kept the Braves winning in the 1990s. "I try to stay away from personal goals, because I feel that so much of this game is failure. It's hard to measure up to those goals," he said in 1995. "My only goal at the beginning of the season is just to be one-ninth of the equation out there every night that hopefully gets us back to the World Series and another win."[2]

*F*ormer President Jimmy Carter and his wife, Rosalyn, are among the celebrities that can occasionally be seen at Braves home games.

FUTURE STARS

The Braves celebrated their 125th year as a franchise in 1996. The team is known in most parts of the world not just for good play, but for playing everywhere. At least, the team plays everywhere on television. Thanks to the cable TV "superstation" of club owner Ted Turner, the Braves are more well-known than most baseball teams.

Part of that recognition comes from an owner who spent nearly two decades worth of time and money before getting his first World Series trophy. Turner has never been shy about spending huge sums for free agents. Some players, like Greg Maddux, were swell investments. Others turned out to be wasted buys. The owner, though, has seemed to count wins more than dollars.

Turner's high-profile media connections have drawn more attention for his team. Marrying actress Jane Fonda has added even more star power to the

Braves. Being in Atlanta, the team gets southern celebrities, like former United States President Jimmy Carter, as notable names in the stands.

Bucks for Baseball

As proof of the collective fame of Turner's team, the Braves were signed to a twenty-year deal to have spring training at Walt Disney World, beginning in 1998. A top tourist attraction would want a top team, to help attract even more visitors. And what better mascot could a team wish for than Mickey Mouse?

The future of major-league teams depends on their available money. Paying the best players costs money. Having a huge cable television deal and a long-term partnership with the Disney Company, assures future dollars for developing new talent and hiring the finest free agents. Likewise, players will want to be a part of a successful tradition like Atlanta's, where there's more chance at some fortune, if not fame. Maddux became the prime example of how a winning tradition in Atlanta is important. He signed a five-year, $28 million deal beginning in 1993, but could have pitched for the Yankees, who offered him $6 million more. Maddux said money wasn't that important, and that he wanted to pitch for a team with the best chance of winning.

Most of all, the Braves have built a solid foundation for future growth: their minor league system. After the 1996 season few fans worried about whether star outfielder David Justice could return healthy. That's because the National League champions had gone on

The Atlanta Braves Baseball Team

*B*raves rookie outfielder Andruw Jones watches his World Series home run leave the yard. At nineteen, Jones was the youngest player to ever homer in World Series play.

*C*hipper Jones and the Indians' Kenny Lofton look to the umpire for the call. After a trade that sent David Justice to the Indians, Lofton joined the Braves for the 1997 season.

with rookie Jermaine Dye, followed by nineteen-year-old sensation Andruw Jones. Whenever a highly-paid veteran on the team has chosen to leave, a younger, more affordable replacement waits in the minors. When third baseman Terry Pendleton decided to sign a free-agent deal with Florida in 1995, his exit simply opened a starting spot for Chipper Jones.

Jones found Atlanta the ideal setting for stardom. Four Atlanta companies hired him to endorse their products. He gained more national attention by advertising Braves games on television and in newspapers.

Spirit of '96

During 1996 the Braves enjoyed another successful season. Led by the strong pitching of John Smoltz, and the clutch hitting of Chipper Jones, the Braves won their division once again. Smoltz finished the year with a record of 24-8, and won the Cy Young Award. Jones blasted 30 home runs and drove in 110, while hitting a robust .309. The Braves reached the World Series, where they fell to the New York Yankees in six games.

The 1996 Olympics gave the Braves a new stadium, and lasting roots in Atlanta. That tradition means a lot to the present and future players. "You ask players around the league, and they really hate to move around from team to team every year. It's kind of a pain, but that's the way the game goes," said third baseman Jones. "Certainly, if the Braves want to keep Chipper Jones around for his entire career, if they think I'm good enough to play in Atlanta for 10–15 years, I'd be more than happy to stay with the Atlanta Braves."[1]

STATISTICS

Team Record

The Braves History

YEARS	LOCATION	W	L	PCT.	PENNANTS	WORLD SERIES
1871–79	Boston	401	128	.758	1877, 1878*	None
1880–89	Boston	575	497	.536	1883*	None
1890–99	Boston	869	508	.631	1891, 1892 1893, 1897, 1898*	None
1900–09	Boston	587	877	.401	None	None
1910–19	Boston	666	815	.450	1914	1914
1920–29	Boston	603	928	.394	None	None
1930–39	Boston	700	829	.458	None	None
1940–49	Boston	719	808	.471	1948	None
1950–59	Boston (1950–52) Milwaukee (1953–59)	854	687	.554	1957–58	1957
1960–69	Milwaukee (1960–65) Atlanta (1966–69)	851	753	.531	None	None
1970–79	Atlanta	725	883	.451	None	None
1980–89	Atlanta	712	845	.457	None	None
1990–96	Atlanta	615	453	.576	1991–92, 1995–96	1995

W=Wins
L=Losses
PCT.=Winning Percentage

PENNANTS=Won league title.
WORLD SERIES=Won World Series.

40

The Atlanta Braves Baseball Team

The Braves Today

YEAR	W	L	PCT.	COACH	DIVISION FINISH
1990	65	97	.401	Russ Nixon Bobby Cox	6
1991	94	68	.580	Bobby Cox	1
1992	98	64	.605	Bobby Cox	1
1993	104	58	.642	Bobby Cox	1
1994	68	46	.596	Bobby Cox	2
1995	90	54	.625	Bobby Cox	1
1996	96	66	.593	Bobby Cox	1

Total History

W	L	PCT.	PENNANTS	WORLD SERIES
8,877	9,011	.496	16	3

Championship Managers

COACH	YEARS COACHED	RECORD	WORLD CHAMPIONSHIPS
Harry Wright	1876–81	254-186	1877, 1878*
John Mornil	1882 1883–88	383-337	1883*
Frank Selee	1890–1901	904-649	1891, 1892, 1893, 1897, 1898*
George Stallings	1913–1920	579-597	1914
Fred Haney	1956–59	341-231	1957
Bobby Cox	1978–81 1990–	856-736	1995

*Won National League championship. The World Series did not begin until 1903.

Great Hitters

						CAREER STATISTICS				
PLAYER	SEA	YRS	G	AB	R	H	HR	RBI	SB	AVG
Hank Aaron	1954–74	21	3,298	12,364	2,174	3,771	755	2,297	240	.305
Rico Carty	1963–72	17	1,651	5,606	712	1,677	204	890	21	.299
Darrell Evans	1969–76 1989	21	2,687	8,973	1,344	2,223	414	1,354	98	.248
Bob Horner	1978–86	10	1,020	3,777	560	1,047	218	685	14	.277
Chipper Jones	1993–	3	305	1,125	203	326	53	196	22	.290
David Justice	1989–96	8	817	2,858	475	786	160	522	33	.275
Kenny Lofton	1997–	6	700	2,821	551	883	39	261	327	.313
Walter Maranville	1912–20 1929–33 1935	23	2,670	10,078	1,255	2,605	28	874	291	.258
Eddie Mathews	1952–66	17	2,391	8,537	1,509	2,315	512	1,453	68	.271
Dale Murphy	1976–90	18	2,180	7,960	1,197	2,111	398	1,266	161	.265

SEA=Seasons with Braves
YRS=Years in the Majors
G=Games
AB=At Bats

R=Runs Scored
H=Hits
HR=Home Runs
RBI=Runs Batted In

SB=Stolen Bases
AVG=Batting Average

Great Pitchers

							CAREER STATISTICS				
PLAYER	SEA	YRS	W	L	PCT.	ERA	G	SV	IP	K	SH
Tom Glavine	1987–	10	139	92	.602	3.46	298	0	1,956	1,212	13
Greg Maddux	1993–	11	165	104	.613	2.87	336	0	2,365	1,643	21
Phil Niekro	1964–83 1987	24	318	274	.537	3.35	864	29	5,404	3,342	45
John Smoltz	1988–	9	114	90	.559	3.45	266	0	1,804	1,528	91
Warren Spahn	1942–64	23	363	245	.597	3.08	750	29	5,246	2,583	63

SEA=Seasons with Braves
YRS=Years in the Majors
W=Wins
L=Losses

PCT.=Winning Percentage
ERA=Earned Runs Average
G=Games
SV=Saves

IP=Innings Pitched
K=Strikeouts
SH=Shutouts

The Atlanta Braves Baseball Team

CHAPTER NOTES

Chapter 1

1. Bob Klapisch, *The World Champion Braves: 125 Years of America's Team* (Kansas City, MO: Andrews & McMeel, 1996), p. 266.

2. "At Last, Atlanta," *USA Today Baseball Weekly,* November 1–7, 1995, p. 13.

Chapter 2

1. Bob Klapisch, *The World Champion Braves: 125 Years of America's Team* (Kansas City, MO: Andrews & McMeel, 1996), p. 207.

Chapter 3

1. *Hank Aaron: Chasing the Dream,* Television documentary, 1996.

2. *Baseball Weekly 1996 Almanac* (Arlington, VA: Gannett Co., 1996), p. 15.

Chapter 4

1. "Ask John Schuerholz," Atlanta Braves World Wide Web page, 1995.

2. Sean Gavitan, "Mr. Low Profile," *Tomahawk,* October 1992, p. 9.

Chapter 5

1. I. J. Rosenberg, *Miracle Season: The Inside Story of the 1991 Atlanta Braves' Race for Baseball Glory* (Atlanta: Turner Publishing), p. 4.

2. Dina Tooley, "Clubhouse Interview: Chipper Jones," Atlanta Braves World Wide Web page, 1995.

Chapter 6

1. "Ask Chipper! Fan Questions to Braves Infielder Chipper Jones," Atlanta Braves World Wide Web page, 1995.

GLOSSARY

ace—The star pitcher on a team's staff.

at-bat—An official time at bat charged to a baseball player. Players are not charged with an at bat if they walk, sacrifice, are hit by a pitch, or reach base on a catcher's interference.

"The Chop Shop"—A nickname for Atlanta-Fulton County Stadium; where the Braves used to play their home games.

ballpark—Another word for a baseball stadium.

clinch—To make final.

diamond—The baseball field.

ERA (Earned Run Average)—The number of earned runs divided by the number of innings pitched multiplied by nine. The ERA is perhaps the best measure of pitching effectiveness.

free agent—A major leaguer whose contractual obligations to his old team have expired and who is free to sign with any major-league team.

Hall of Fame—Located in Cooperstown, N.Y; membership in the National Baseball Hall of Fame is the highest honor that can be awarded to a professional player.

homer—A home run.

infielder—Someone who plays an infield position (first, second, or third base, or shortstop).

knuckleball—A pitch gripped with the pitcher's knuckles. The pitched ball has very little rotation and dives or moves suddenly near the plate.

League Championship Series (LCS)—The best-of-seven series that determines the American and National League champions.

majors—The major leagues of professional baseball. They are the American League and the National League.

MVP Award—Most Valuable Player Award.

The Atlanta Braves Baseball Team

National League—The first professional baseball league; the National League was founded in 1876.

outfielder—Someone who plays an outfield position (right field, center field, or left field).

Peachtree Street—The main street in downtown Atlanta, Georgia.

pennant—A league championship, also called the flag.

player's strike—A work stoppage by the players in order to get the owners to comply with their demands.

reliever—A relief pitcher. Relievers come into the game if the starting pitcher is unable to complete it.

spitballer—A pitcher who throws the ball after it has been moistened with saliva or sweat. Throwing a spitball is an illegal pitch.

sports psychologist—A doctor that cares for the mental health of athletes.

"30/30"—This describes a player who has hit thirty home runs and stolen thirty bases in the same season.

triple A—The highest level of baseball's minor leagues.

wild card—The club with the best won-lost percentage in regular season play of the teams that were not division winners. The wild card team in each league earns a chance for postseason play.

World Series—The end of the season best-of-seven series that pits the champions of the National and American leagues against each other. Also known as the Fall Classic.

FURTHER READING

Buege, Bob. *The Milwaukee Braves: A Baseball Eulogy.* Milwaukee: Douglas American Sports Publications, 1988.

Deane, Bill. *Top 10 Baseball Hitters.* Springfield, N.J.: Enslow Publishers, Inc., 1998.

————. *Top 10 Baseball Home Run Hitters.* Springfield, N.J.: Enslow Publishers, Inc., 1997.

Klapisch, Bob, and Van Wieren, Pete. *The World Champion Braves: 125 Years of America's Team.* Atlanta: Turner Publishing, 1996.

Rosenberg, I. J. *Miracle Season!* Atlanta: Turner Publishing, 1991.

Savage, Jeff. *Deion Sanders: Star Athlete.* Springfield, N.J.: Enslow Publishers, Inc., 1996.

Sink, Richard. *Chop to the Top.* Cornelius, N.C.: Tomahawk Press, 1992.

Thornley, Stew. *Sports Great Greg Maddux.* Springfield, N.J.: Enslow Publishers, Inc., 1997.

Zack, Bill. *Tomahawked.* New York: Simon and Schuster, 1993.

The Atlanta Braves Baseball Team

INDEX

WHERE TO WRITE

Atlanta Braves
P.O. Box 4064
Atlanta, GA 30302

WEBSITE

http://www.atlantabraves.com